REFLECTIONS
OF
GOD'S LOVE

REFLECTIONS
OF
GOD'S LOVE

Poems And Verse

Illustrations by:
KEITH FURLONG
and
JANET FURLONG

authorHOUSE®

AuthorHouse™
1663 Liberty Drive
Bloomington, IN 47403
www.authorhouse.com
Phone: 1-800-839-8640

Published by AuthorHouse   06/19/2012

ISBN: 978-1-4685-8610-7 (sc)
ISBN: 978-1-4685-8611-4 (e)

Contents

Chapter 1

GOD'S CALLING

When we're first called to follow Jesus Christ and make Him our personal Saviour, there are lots of questions we usually want to ask. The poems in this first chapter, cover some of these questions from different points of view. God has laid out a plan for us all to follow. The Way, The Truth and The Life and a prayer that Jesus taught his disciples, the prayer we know as, "The Lord's Prayer". I hope you enjoy these poems and are blest by them.

God's Calling

Born into a Christian home,
raised into the church of God,
sung His praises said my prayers
doing what I thought He'd want.
Sometimes I thought I heard God's voice,
but never sure, ignored the call,
and surely as the years went by
I drifted back into the world.
Yet deep inside I loved my Lord
and knew one day I would be called
to do His work and walk His way.
The years went by and nothing came
the days the weeks were all the same,
doing all the world did do,
yet nothing Lord I did for You.
My earthly father whom I loved
more dearly than another soul
and whom I prayed would never die,
yet, one day God called him home.
A curate from the church did call
and there upon that very day,
invited, I did accept the call
and gave my very heart away,
to Jesus Christ my Saviour, Lord,
and gave my life to live His word.
And from that moment to this time
 and born again I have no choice
but listen to the heavenly call,
obeying when I hear God's voice
and going where my dear Lord sends,

to take His word into the world
to turn God's enemies into friends
and shows how Jesus loves them all.
My wife and I were surely given
a call from God, a task from Heaven,
and one day when our work is done
and God will surely take us home,
then someone else will carry on
until God's work on earth we've won.

Is A Christian?

Is a Christian someone who was baptised in a font?
And to the church on Sunday goes,
or is it all a front,
to show the world how good you are,
all dressed in Sunday best,
not drinking, smoking, swearing,
so the neighbours are impressed?
Or is a Christian someone who,
upon their knees does pray,
asking God for all good things
for each and every day?
A big new house, a shiny car,
designer is the name
and lots of money in the bank,
this surely is the game.
Oh God is good, or so it seems,
He gives you everything,
a lovely wife, a smashing life,
His praises shall you sing.
But what about when things go wrong
and troubles lie ahead,
do you still praise our Saviour's name
whilst lying on your bed?
When sleep won't come and all alone
and everything is gone,
can you still pray and thank your God
for everything He's done, or do you say,
what is this thing that you have done to me,
why did you take the gifts away,
how can this really be?

I trusted you and prayed each night
for all good things to see,
why did you steal all them away
and bring me poverty?
Or is a Christian someone who,
when praying on his knees,
has no concern for his own life,
but for the world he sees.
He firstly thanks you for his wife
who gives him love and shows,
compassion for the people
who have nothing and who knows,
that God will love you always
and never let you go.
He then prays for others
who God has brought to mind,
the deaf, the blind, the crippled
and all the ones you'll find,
in all the foreign countries
no one cares about,
hungry, homeless children,
so raise your voice and shout,
help them Lord and bring to them
the people who still care,
share the name of Jesus Christ
to everybody there.
Now if you think you're Christian
and Christ is in your heart,
then you can make a difference,
but first you have to start,

to pray again and look beyond,
your needs, that God already knows,
and pray for other people,
it's up to you to choose,
and once you take your eyes of self
and focus them on Him,
you'll really make a difference
and never feel the same,
and God will bless you when you put
the other people first,
and know that you're a Christian
and you are truly blest.

The Atheist

Why should I believe, like you?
there is a God on high,
for all I see is tragedy and ask the question, why?
Are children dying every day,
starvation is the norm,
I don't believe there is a God,
or He would keep them free from harm.
On the news most every day,
another disaster is on the way,
so if there is a God it's clear,
when trouble comes He's nowhere near.
Why did He let that person die?
Why does He let the children cry?
when parents they are dead and gone
and they are left there on their own,
when He could keep them free from harm?
Why are there fights and yobs and louts?
I hear the non believers shouts,
for if there is a God,
then why? Are little babies born then die.
"If miracles are true then why?
does anybody need to cry,
I'm sick I'm ill, I'm full of pain,
I'm off to the doctors once again."
A sunami, lots of people dead,
huge tidal waves destroyed their homes,
and I've already said,
I don't believe! with moans and groans.
So, from an atheist's point of view,
there is no God for me and you,

what doom and gloom his words portray,
I'm glad I don't see things his way,
for God created all we see
and I just know that when we pray,
He listens both to you and me.
And when things happen we don't choose
and illness comes and causes pain
there is no reason we should lose,
for God will make us well again.
It is not God that makes things bad,
or children cry or people sad,
or hungry, like the atheist said,
or cause disasters so they're dead.
It is a fact that man does sin and sin and sin and sin again
and that's the reason we feel pain,
so God did send His Son to die so we might start to live again.
So if we believe what God declares,
then when this life on earth is done,
 Eternal life for all He shares,
if we believe in Jesus name.
So listen Mr Atheist,
please read God's word and He'll convict,
you of the truth that's free from sin and even you can start again.
Then one day when your life is done,
our God will come and take you home.

Do You Believe

Do you believe there is a God, Creator of the world?

Do you believe He died for us that we might all be saved?

Do you believe He rose from death and victory He brought,
to one and all who believe His name, for those who never doubt?

Do you believe He's by your side when you cry out His name?

Do you believe He forgives your sins when all you feel is shame?

Do you believe He loves you more than anyone can do?

Do you believe He's always there wherever you may go?

Do you believe He knows your heart and every breath you take?

Do you believe He knows your mind and every move you make?

Do you believe when you cry those tears, He's there to wipe them dry?

Do you believe He gives you rest in green pastures there to lie?

Do you believe that one day soon together we will be,
to walk with Him and talk with Him in perfect harmony?
If you believe in all these things then never doubt nor fear,
for just as surely as He lives, He will make all things clear,
and one day soon with bad times past His purpose to fulfil,
then you and I will start again and stay within God's will,
and all He asks of you and me is to openly receive,
His mercy, love and tenderness and that we will believe.

If God Did Not Exist

I can't imagine life on earth
if God did not exist,
for what would life be all about
for many poor souls.
Born into a life of poverty,
hunger, pain and strife,
everything so meaningless
without Eternal life.
So what's the point of living
many people say,
if all I do is hunger
each and every day.
My children cry thro lack of food
no clothes, or bed on which to rest,
nothing to improve our lot
is this the very best?
Yet all I know is God sees all
and feels the pain you do
and if you will only seek His face,
He'll surely help you through.
Then one day when your time has come
for God to call you home,
He'll welcome you with open arms
to a life you've never known.
For God's eternal resting home is
everything you've missed,
for there would be no point to life,
if God did not exist.

Is There Anybody Out There

Is there anybody out there that would sacrifice their son for me?
Is there anybody who would nail their son upon a tree,
to set me free?
Is there anybody who would pay the ultimate price for my sin
and choose to die so that I might start again?
Yet one man did and died for me,
He hung and bled upon that rugged tree,
forgave my sins and set me free, to live again and praise
His wondrous name, to follow Him, not sharing in His pain
but rejoicing in His victory, because He died and rose again.
Yes, Jesus is my Saviour, the Son of God set free,
to live again and by His Spirit dwell in you and me.
So if anybody's out there that believes in Jesus' name?
Confess your sins and follow Him, you'll never be the same.
For Jesus is the Son of God, accept Him as your Saviour
and you will live and reign with Him for always and forever.

Draw Close To Him In Prayer

Sometimes it's really hard to pray
and hard to say what's on your mind,
we don't know where to go
or know just where we'll find
that inner peace communing brings
when being close to God,
and knowing that He hears our prayers
and requests that we have made.
Yet, when we find that quiet time
to spend alone with Him,
and sit awhile and listen
to that voice from deep within.
And knowing Father hears the words
before they're even said,
and knows our very thoughts
going on inside our head.
For all our precious Father wants
is for us to sit and talk,
and tell Him what we really think
of how our daily walk, thro life,
has brought us to this place
where we can feel so near to Him
and by His wondrous grace,
a new life can begin.
So when you don't know what to say,
just thank our God for giving us
the greatest gift that one could give,
His Son, a sacrifice in love,
and drawing close in prayer to Him.

The Way, The Truth And The Life

I am the Way so follow Me and I will lead you to my Father,
or no-one else can guide you there or promise you a life forever,

I am the Truth of God revealed, the heart of God as seen in Me,
was born again, in resurrection, set you free.

I am the Life, the Spirit given, to live in you and guide you on,
the straight and narrow path to Heaven, Eternal life for you I won.

I am the Way, the Truth, the Life, believe in Me, I am God's
Son and I will live in you forever and prepare for you your
Eternal home.

Heaven's Gates

When I arrive at Heavens gates
who will be there to see me in?
For if it's true what I've been told
then I'll be judged on all my sins.
I truly know God's word for-tells
that we can choose to live or die,
to live in Heaven or rot in hell
 believe in Christ do not deny,
for those that choose to turn away
and set their hearts against our Lord,
when they arrive and gates are closed
they'll wish that they had read God's
word.
So all believers enter in
and stand before the judgement seat,
and when our Lord has judged our sins
then we can worship at His feet.
It all seems fairly clear to me
if we believe in Jesus name,
from now unto Eternity
our lives will never be the same.

One day when our God calls us home
and we arrive at Heaven's gates,
I know who waits to let me in
the one who died for all our sakes.
So never fear the judgement seat
for Jesus washed our sins away,
and when we worship at His feet
and there upon that glorious day,
no more remembers what we've done
no-one not even God's own Son,
for I know Jesus stands and waits
to welcome me to Heaven's gates.

The Lord's Prayer

Jesus said that when you pray,
Pray to Father God
He taught His disciples what to say
And here's the words He taught.

'Our Father who art in heaven
and hallowed be thy name'

He's our paternal need,
so love Him just the same.

'Your Kingdom come,
Your will be done, on earth
as it is in Heaven'
and on earth in us He'll reign.

'Give us this day our daily bread'
and feed us as You may.

'And forgive us our trespasses,
as we forgive those that trespass against us'
are words that Jesus gave
to take our sins away.

'and lead us not into temptation,
but deliver us from evil'
and keep us safe from harm
and protect us from the devil.

'For yours is the Kingdom
the Power and the Glory forever,
Amen.

CHAPTER 2

GOD'S FAITHFULNESS

When we first believe, we have to trust that Jesus will guide our lives. We take our walk with Jesus in faith, for unlike the disciples of Jesus, we cannot see Him in person. We can, although, feel the presence of our Lord and Saviour and the more we stand in Faith, the stronger the reality of God's presence in our lives becomes.

By Faith

If faith is what we hope for in certain purity,
 then hope is being certain of what we cannot see.
By faith, the bible tells us and so we understand
that all the universe was formed by God's Eternal hand,
and everything we see was made, not by those things perceived
and not by those things visible, but by faith we have received.
Again the bible tells us of the great men gone before,
whose faith we can believe in for we know that it is so.
There is Abel, Enoch and there's Noah
a man of faith we can be sure,
who built an ark at God's command
he built the boat upon dry land,
and all the people laughed and scorned
but faithful Noah had been for-warned.
An inheritance, from God, Abraham received
and by faith the barren Sarah, knew not how she had conceived.
And if you understand God's word and know, by faith,
these men were driven, and lived their lives by what they heard, and
promises that they were given.
And Isaac, Jacob, Joseph too, Moses and Gideon
to name but a few,
all men so driven by God's command
all striving for the promised land.
Yet all commended for their faith, and yet no promises did gain but
in perfection, we as they, God did plan another day.
When all together we will be and live for all Eternity
with all those saints and men of faith,
we thank our God that by His grace
and our belief in His dear Son,
our place we'll gain in God's Eternal home.

Read Hebrews Ch11

Stand In Faith

We stand in faith as believers
of our one true God.
We stand firm upon the rock of Christ.
No-one can shake us or persuade us
from then truth.
No-one can blind our eyes or lead us
from the path to Eternal life,
if we stand in faith.

How Deep Is Faith

How deep inside your heart is faith?
Faith to trust in and believe
that Jesus died and rose again,
and all His miracles can you and I perceive,
that written in the Word is given, a text,
that says He gives to you
the power to do the things He did,
and even greater works than these
have you the faith to dare believe?
How deep is faith within your heart?
are you prepared His love to show?
And if He calls you by His word
are you prepared to go?
Your love for Jesus you confess,
by faith, to others would proclaim,
if they believed in Jesus Christ,
their lives would never be the same.
And if your faith the jeering stand
and bitter words that come from man
and those that don't believe it's true,
how deep will your faith, for Jesus go?
And when you've answered yes,
to questions of your faith we've given,
then Jesus will, one day by faith,
prepare for you a home in Heaven.

Healed By Faith

A woman ill for many years
such pain she must have suffered,
there seemed there was no hope for her
until she then discovered,
a man named Jesus was around
and people flocked to see Him,
for stories of this may abound
of illnesses he'd cure them.
So risking life she struggled through
the crowds until she saw Him,
and then she touched His garment hem
and Jesus knew it was her.
For power flowed from His body
and standing in that place,
He said, you know I've healed you
and saved you through your faith.
For twelve long years she'd been so ill
until she heard of Jesus,
let's be like her and touch His hem,
in faith He's sure to heal us.

Keep The Faith

Such faith have I to trust in God
that every day He'll walk with me,
and when life's pressures crowd on in
its then my God by power will be,
so close to help me through each day
to give me strength and hold my hand,
and through the desert of life's way
He'll guide me to the promised land,
where milk and honey surely flow
and peace and tranquillity I will know,
and in the joy of God's pure grace
we are encouraged to keep the faith.

How Can You Know

How can you know or understand
the truth impressed upon my soul,
my heart awash with yearning deep within
a time gone by of hours spent alone with Christ,
washed and cleansed released from torment
not judged but freed from all my guilt and shame.
To meditate upon God's word
and try to understand the reason why,
when straying from the path of life
to wander from a truth proclaimed
so blinded by temptation, appearing not to lie.
So listen to that heavenly voice calling out to you,
offering a guiding hand to bring you back in view
of all that He has promised and surely will fulfil,
if you will keep your faith in Him
and carry out His will,
enduring as the faithful
the ones that's gone before,
the patriarchs and witnesses and many, many more.
Now just as then we keep the faith,
enduring to the end,
ensuring that we run the race
and one day He will send us to that valiant victory
and when the trial's done,
we'll raise our voice in one accord
and praise our God we've won.

God's Faithfullness

God's chosen people cried for help and to their rescue came,
a leader He did choose for them and Moses was his name.
To do the things that Moses did and lead the people out
from misery and anguish to me there is no doubt,
that when God calls and chooses you His purpose to fulfil
He'll give you everything you need to carry out His will.
When to the Red sea Moses came and all the people cried,
the waters deep we cannot cross unto the other side.
But God was there and knew that when, the Red sea He had parted,
the Israelites would in safety cross, not one was lost that started.
And when the chariots did cross in close pursuit did follow,
the waters closed upon their heads, not one did see tomorrow.
So onward thro the desert all the people followed on,
as God did lead them day by day and they all trusted Him,
for thro the day a cloud of dust, a pillar of fire by night,
to guide the people on their way, to guide them in their plight,
and many times the miracles, God did surely show
and leading them all forward to where, they did not know.
He fed them with the bread from Heaven, bitter waters He made
sweet and even when they still complained, God provided meat.
Upon the Mount of Sinai, God's laws He gave for them
but the Israelites had turned from Him when Moses did return.
A second time, God wrote the laws, on stone for them to follow and
punished those who chose to sin and gave them all great sorrow.
Now when they reached the promised land, the people would not
enter, so for many years in the desert they lived and God gave them
a new leader.

And it's here I end the story this far
and the moral for all is quite clear,
if you trust in God and follow when called
you need never doubt or fear,
for He'll lead you on, till His work you have done
and the land that He promised you'll gain,
by trusting His Son, new life you have won
and Eternal salvation you'll claim.

God's Saving Grace

If we have the love of Christ in our hearts
and the grace of God to lead us on,
what more can we ask for our lives here on earth, till the breath in
our bodies is done.
What more can we say to the rest of the world,
to a people who know not our Lord
and whose lives without love, of our Saviour above, will one day be
drawn to His word.
For our God is so real and His presence is felt
everyday He holds us so near,
and our lives He fills with compassion and love
and the name of Jesus drives away fear.
So when a knock on the door of your heart is felt
then please open and let our Lord in,
for He'll give you such peace and such joy
and release you from all guilt and shame.
And no good things that you've done
and no favours you've given,
no good works or kind deeds that you've shown
for it's only by grace of our dear precious Lord,
that will one day save you for Heaven.

Jesus Is The Only Way

Jesus is the only way
my future in His hands,
I look to Him to guide my paths
included in His plans.
For you and I can put our trust
in all we say and do,
and pray each day His guiding hand
the way for us He'll show.

Don't fear the world and all its ways
so hard for us to bear,
just look to Him who knows it all
and with us He will share,
His love for each and everyone
our burdens He will carry,
and give us back our joy, His peace
and all that He has promised.

He gave us life, He gives us hope
no moment should we worry,
just putting all our trust in Him
not looking for tomorrow,
but living for the here and now
together we should pray
that soon my love we'll be as one
and knowing in that day,
that victory He'll win for us
because we keep our faith
and put our trust in Jesus Christ
who brought us to this place.

So hold my hand let's follow Him
and stay so close together,
bonded by eternal love
that will endure forever,
and may we never fail to say
that Jesus is the only way.

We 've Won

Oh what joy to behold and to stand before the throne of grace,
the pictures of our Lord unfold as we meet our Saviour Face to face.
But until that day we must believe and never let our faith subside,
for, if somehow, we are deceived, then we will never be His bride.
So stand firm and put your armour on and protect yourself from fiery
darts,
armed with the sword of the Spirit, we cannot fail, to trust in the
name of God's own Son.
Then, when Jesus calls you home and you know you ran the race
with pride,
you'll live for all Eternity with all those that's gone before,
and standing by His side,
rejoicing in the victory, we will proclaim we've won.

Chapter 3

LIFE'S EXPERIENCES

Sometimes in life we can stand in a crowded room and yet feel so alone. The pressures of life grow stronger and storm clouds seem to gather. Yet thro all the turmoil God stays with us, always faithful, always sure, always there, ready to reach down and pick us up when we fall and to carry us when we are tired and weary. He's always there ready to Make Everything Right.

The Dream

Sometimes we dream, our dreams are strange
we try to reason why they seem,
we try to reason why this dream
is real enough but somehow seems,
so strange in all we dream.
Our mind is greater than we think
our dreams are visions, there to see,
of all we know, of all we bring
is this the way it's meant to be?
Or are our dreams a play on words
with visions seeming so absurd
or our dreams in life to see
or are our dreams reality?
If God gives dreams for men to dream,
and young men visions so it seems,
then please dear God release me now
so for my dream I'll show you how,
that God in all His wisdom meant
my dream for all the world is sent,
but no-one seems my dream will care
or to explain my dream will share,
so please dear God just show me how,
that in my dream the here and now,
is given for us all to share
and showing that we all do care,
for everyone that hears my dream
you'll show to them just how it seems,
and when this life on earth is done
and into Heaven, we call our home,
my dream will surely show you how
that tho I'm old, the here and now,
is all that this is meant to be
a dream of pure reality.

What Is Beauty

For you
What is beauty but a reflection of one's soul
that calm reflection of an inner peace,
a look of gentleness telling all
bringing mind and body unto rest.

For them
What use that look, attractive tho it seems
if deep within they plan but to deceive,
capturing the heart of man
enticing him by subtle glance.
Drawn by outward signs
unknowing why they take that chance,
but once ensnared nothing they can do
but hope that someday they will find true love.

For you
And here, my love, is where I come to you
describing all my heart employs,
for in your face I see the radiance of a heavenly host,
a beauty that needs no adornment
but surely is the most acceptable to all,
for there within that smile
and eyes that shine
and show the serenity of our God,
a peace that permeates my heart with love
that only you can give.
Attracted by a kiss
that takes me far from worldly cares,
and enfolded in your arms
pure bliss.
No words can mans oration bring
or justify the beauty given you
by our Creator God and King.

A Prayer For Help

Why do I feel this way O'Lord,
why do I feel this way,
tired and lonely, feel no-one is caring,
anxious and frightened sometimes despairing,
please help me O'Lord I pray.
Each day goes by so slowly
all seeming much the same,
no-one to talk to, no-one to blame,
can't look to the future, just live in the past,
sitting and waiting, how long will this last?
There's always an answer to all of our woes
and Jesus will help you, your troubles He knows.
He will help you and guide you and show you the way,
just teach out and ask Him, just reach out and pray.
Lord Jesus you know me you've called me by name,
You've looked deep inside me, you've seen all my pain.
I know You can help me and show me the way,
I know when I ask you, I'll not be the same.
So please dear Lord Jesus forgive all my sin,
I've opened my heart, so please enter in
and stay by my side each night and each day,
renew me, refresh me, God bless me I pray.

God Reached In

The storm it raged, all hope had gone,
my mind was tossed and torn,
I knew not where I was or what I'd done,
hopelessly lost I staggered on.
Deeper and deeper into the mire I fell,
was this my life pictured before me,
was this the way to hell.
The dark clouds rolled, the thunder roared,
it's ceaseless noise made no escape.
Deeper and deeper and on I fell,
my God, my God what have I done?
There's no way out, I see no way,
as down and down I go,
the darkness all enveloping,
I see the sins I've borne.
The heart ache, misery and anguish that I've caused
deserving of all scorn.
Yet in the turmoil, tossed and torn,
God reaches down and in His arms I'm borne.
I care for you my child, He says,
you tried to hide your face from me
and fell into this dark, dark hole of sin and misery.
You tried to run and hide your face,
the shame, the pain, your own disgrace,
no thoughts for those you left behind
but I did seek and here I found,
a wretch not worthy of My grace,
yet I have brought you to this place
of recognising who you are,
before you wandered off too far.

I've reached and saved you from that pit,
a place no child of mine, not fit
for all my purpose not fulfilled,
the journey not complete,
but from the dark into the light,
I've brought you to My feet.
So rest a while and seek My face,
I'll give you peace and rest
and wonder on the words I've said,
and do your very best,
to show her that the day will come
when you will both be blest.

A Tear

A tear rolled slowly down your cheek
my heart it stopped and missed a beat,
and as I gazed into your eyes
it was then that I realised,
that looking back from deep within
convicting me of all my sin,
with love, compassion, saving grace
I looked and saw within your face,
the glory of our gracious Lord
and as you stood there without word
I saw another tear emerge,
this time the welling in your eye
surpassed all others gone before,
my soul was crying, calling out
for the tears I cry there is no doubt,
are the tears of blood shed deep within
convicting me of all my sin.
Atonement on that cross He made
His blood He shed for you and me,
for all our sins He died just there
He died that we all might be free.
What misery and pain I've caused
I turned my back on my dear Lord.
The suffering and pain You took
for now I see it in that look.
Another tear rolls down your cheek
and yet again you do not speak,
my guilt, my shame my soul does cry
the tears I cannot wipe them dry.
And yet my God His love pours out

His grace and mercy freedom shout,
convicting me no more to sin
my heart must let the Lord pour in.
Another tear it rolled on down,
and stopped before it reached your chin,
this time the look but with a smile,
but still convicting me of sin.
What must I do to make things right,
to dry the tears and make you smile?
Go sin no more is what you shout
and then I'll let my love pour out.
I don't deserve the love you show
I'll go away and sin no more.
The lord go with me then one day
when He's wiped the tears away,
I pray that we can start again
and that I'll cause you no more pain.

Born Again

We start our life so safe and warm
snuggled in our mother's womb,
and there we stay until we're born,
free from troubles safe from harm.
Then in those years a babe in arms
loved and cherished growing older,
till the day we take our leave
and in the world it's burdens shoulder.
Yet striving on no fears or doubts
working in a world that shouts,
gain more success and earn more money
to buy the things the world can offer.
On and on we keep on striving
fancy cars and bigger houses,
borrow more for there's no losers.
Then one day the doubt's creep in
the worlds attractions lost their charm,
sliding backwards full of worry
I'm in trouble lost my money.
The days have gone when I felt safe,
I've lost it all and I've no place
to run or hide conceal my shame,
dry my tears, I feel such pain.
I don't know which way to turn,
but then in darkness all alone,
I feel the hand of God reach in
taking me from sinking sand,
set my feet on solid ground.
I've put my trust in Jesus Christ
and know that from this moment on

no more to fear I'm not alone
the worlds attractions they're all gone.
The things that used to pull me in
the things that caused my soul to sin,
I'm free at last to carry on.
The morale of this tale is clear,
to lead a life that's free from fear
a life that's free from guilt and sin,
when our Lord knocks then let Him in.
Then once more as that unborn babe,
so warm and snug and free from harm,
born again but this time safe
until the day He calls you home.

The Heavenly Light

I awoke and there before me stood
a light so bright I could not bear to look,
but not afraid I spoke and asked the reason why,
am I to live or am I soon to die?
Just look at me, a voice proclaimed,
angelic on an earthly plane,
be not afraid for you will understand
that I am here to guide you through your life
and keep you safe from doubt and fear
until a time not known, until a time,
when our Almighty Father calls you home.
I chose to look upon a face,
so radiant and yet so full of understanding,
compassion, love and grace, of mercy,
tenderness and all consuming power
that made me feel so safe.
The light remained and held my gaze
tho no longer could I see the heavenly face,
yet held by energy,
transfixed upon that place
aware that the face I'd seen had once before
upon Damascus road, made clear,
the face I knew was our dear Lord.
Then I became the light,
the light absorbed inside of me,
was then I understood what this was meant to be.
The spirit of our Lord, a gift we all assumed,
was given to help and guide us on our journey
through this life and on our journey into Heaven.
Yet now I see that in our darkest hour

when soul and spirit feel void and helpless,
despairing, crying with remorse,
it's then the Holy Spirit power,
the light of life, that energy that only God controls,
absorbs into our very being, absorbs into our very souls.

A New Life In Me

How long must I carry this burden Lord,
how long must I carry on,
dreaming a dream of things to come
how long till the battles won.
The enemies rage, the fight goes on
my strength ebbs slowly away,
as I weary I close my eyes to sleep
and wait for another day.
But there in the darkness of the night
a voice calls out to me,
fight on fight on till the battle is won
fight on to the victory.
I hung on a cross and the people they mocked
the sins of the world on Me laid,
I hung till the life ebbed away from my soul
I hung till the debt it was paid.
So whatever you've done
I will stand by you son,
and will walk by your side all the way.
Fear not when it seems so hard for to bear
and your burden so hard for to carry,
remember I'm there and your burden I'll share
don't fear, don't panic, don't worry.
The road might seem long and the end not in sight
but soon you'll remember I said,
when I died on that cross the battle was won
for three days and I rose from the dead.
So when the battle you've won
and a victory claimed
and the burden you've carried has gone,
remember to praise and to glorify God
and a new life that you've just begun.

Make Everything Right

There are times in your life when things go wrong
and no one seems to care,
but if you turn to God and ask for His help
your troubles He will share.
He'll ask you what's wrong and why you're so sad
and you're getting depressed, are things really that bad.
For there in God's word a solution is found
for it says that you should never worry,
for God will take care and your burden He'll bear
if you truly trust Him to carry.
So take on His yoke and read what He says
that His burden is light and is best,
and thro Him you'll discover you need never worry
and your soul will surely find rest.
For Jesus is gentle and lowly in heart
so stay by His side day and night
and you will discover that Jesus our Saviour
in time will make everything right.

Trust In Me

I can't express the way that I feel
the gratitude from deep within,
forgiveness, love and open arms
to help me thro my guilt and shame.
What more can God His love to show
with arms outstretched, His mercy shown.
The loving smile the warm embrace
the words you speak, show Gods true grace.
I once was blind but now I see
are words of true reality.
My heart explodes with love for you,
I wait to see what God will do,
and pray that someday soon my love
in all His mercy shown for us,
together once again we'll be
for in your heart you'll surely know,
and with your eyes you'll surely see
that you can put your trust in me.

Chapter 4

ETERNAL HOME

This chapter covers a variety of poems, some taken from scripture and some about the reality of life. Striving to better our lives and provide more luxuries for our families, we sometimes, lose focus of the plan God has for our lives. We wander off the straight and narrow path, and it's then we have to call on Jesus to bring us back into the guiding plan He has for us. We should always be guided by His hand, following His word until the day we reach our Eternal home with Jesus.

I Don't Understand

I don't understand why man fights man
and wars and famine are caused,
God gave this earth for all to share
and that's what He first proposed.
All equal in right the young and the old,
to care for each other,
that's what we are told.
So then what went wrong to cause such
a mess for people to weep and live in such stress,
to live out their lives in hunger and
strife when God gave this land,
I don't understand.
Oh how I yearn for a world full of peace,
where we all love each other
in a world with no grief,
in a world where we share all our food
and all things,
in a world where we care
and God's love to us brings,
a true understanding of life here on earth,
where God truly shows us
what we're really worth,
all the treasures in heaven
or the treasures on earth,
can't buy what He's given
to us by the birth,
of our Saviour for heaven,
Jesus our Lord,
it's this that He's given
declared by His word.

God's Champion

He stood there nearly ten feet tall
a giant of a man,
a champion of the Philistines
he stood six cubits and a span.
A bronze helmet worn upon his head
and clothed in a coat of mail,
the spear, the very size of it
made everybody wail.
He shouted to the army,
the servant's of king Saul,
send out your men to fight me
and I will slay them all.
Everyone was sore afraid
and knew not what to do,
when David, son of Jesse, proclaimed,
this man I'll kill for you.
David strode out with staff in hand,
five pebbles in his bag,
and stood before Goliath
which made the giant mad.
Who is this boy
you've sent to me?
and cursed him by his god's
but David knew that very soon
he'd make him eat his words.
Then David loaded up his sling
and aimed it at his head
and when it struck Goliath,
he fell on his face to earth.
The philistines knew that he was dead.
 David cut off Goliath's head
so everyone could see,
that when you have God on your side
you'll claim the victory.

Heaven's Call

A new born baby dies
it seems such needless pain,
we ask the question why?
Yet our God, Creator of all life
receives the child into His arms
it's life for all eternity,
a cherub earthly sent
but for Heaven meant.
Young men, healthy as the world perceives,
yet taken in their prime
God's purpose to fulfil,
we seek for answers
yet our Lord does call them home,
according to His will.
Wise men, whose lives on earth
have taught us how to live,
and as like wise men gone before
their lives for us they gave,
in strict obedience
to the calling of His Word.
Old men, whose lives on earth they spent,
searching for the truth
and trying hard to understand
the reason they were sent,
for tho they tried so very hard,
God's purpose to achieve,
no- one but Him who sent us
can call us to believe.
Yet one day we will meet as one
from babies to the very old,
and there before the throne of God
we'll see the truth that's been foretold,
and meet our God
who's waiting for us all
when we respond to Heaven's call.

Is Anybody Out There

In the world right now
and every second gone, and yet to come
I see the hungry children,
a consequence of how their lives began.
Born into a rich world
yet poverty in this place beyond compare
and those with much to give
could these help these little ones
if only they would care.
Oh yes I know, appeals are made
and money given,
and some of it may reach these children,
yet no amount can buy a place in Heaven.
For no one yet has told them
that Jesus is their friend,
and knowing Him and loving Him,
a love that never ends.
Is anybody out there
to show these kids God's love,
and give the kind of caring
that comes from Heaven above.

New Life For You And Me

Jesus wore the simplest clothes
sandals on His feet,
nowhere to really call His home
nothing much to eat.
Yet, He never once complained
or sought for richer gain,
for Jesus was the Son of God
and for us all He came,
to live on earth as man did live
and teach the world to love,
and prove by His great miracles
the power came from above.
But just as now the greed of man
and jealousy was rife
and tho's of whom He came to save
demanded of His life.
They hung Him on a wooden tree
His life it ebbed away,
yet still our Lord and Saviour
fills our lives today.
For Jesus died and rose again
to claim a victory
and bring us all salvation,
new life for you and me.

I Have No Time

I have no time I'm late for work,
I'll pray when I get home,
I have no time to go to church
for all the hours have gone.
I have no time to thank my God
for all He's done for me,
I'm busy now my friends have come
I've got to make them tea.
I have no time to help or care
for others people's lives,
I have no time to stop and share
with husbands or their wives.
I have no time to eat my food
or sleep till late at night,
I have no time to even dream,
I'm in a desperate plight.
My life is full of working hard
and striving for the best,
and that is why I have no time
to stop or even rest.
Yet if tomorrow I should die
I don't know what I'd do,
if I met Jesus and He said
'I have no time for you'.

Cry For Joy

When Jesus hung upon a cross
and suffered all that grief and pain,
the sky went black and lightning struck
and all the people felt the rain,
but no-one knew that high above
ten thousand angels cried,
for they had seen the agony
and watched until He died.
Their Lord they loved so very much
no sin in Him was found,
for Jesus was the Son of God
the Saviour of mankind.
And so the angel's tears they flowed
and washed away the blood,
that ran from Jesus' body
to where the people stood,
and when at last the rain did cease
the tears God wiped them dry,
and He did tell the angels
to sing and glorify.
For very soon the one they'd seen
gasping for His breath,
would rise again to new life
for God rebuked His death,
and then ten thousand angels
the tears would once more flow,
but now instead of sorrow
the angels cried for joy.

Share His Word

I walked alone, no-one in sight,
I felt at peace my heart was free,
I'd been rescued from my plight
when I let Jesus walk with me.
I used to strive to be the best
always trying to beat the rest.
A better job, a bigger car,
working hard so I'd go far.
My family I rarely saw
yet still I wanted more and more,
until one day I collapsed in pain
my heart gave out couldn't take the strain.
I'd worked so hard, now lost it all,
everything gone, I stood alone
no-one cared, was on my own.
I knelt and prayed, please help me Lord
I know I've led a life of sin,
and Jesus standing on His word
forgave it all and entered in.
I now walk free and so can you,
let Jesus show you what to do,
my life has changed, I praise my Lord
so stand with me and share His word.

Will I Get To Heaven

Will I get to Heaven
if all my life I've been,
a kind and friendly person
to everyone I've seen.
And will I get to Heaven,
if to the poor I've given money
and to the hungry people,
I've fed them bread and honey.
And will I get to Heaven
if I've never told a lie,
and never said an unkind word
or made a person cry.
And will I get to Heaven
if my thoughts I've kept them pure,
and never mixed with people
of whom I'm not quite sure.
And will I get to Heaven
if all my life I've spent,
in service for the needy
and those that people sent,
for me to love and care for
and do my very best,
to try to make them well again
and give the weary rest.
Or is there something missing
that I really need to do,
like asking God into my life
because He died for me and you,
and believing that He rose again
and lives inside of me,
then yes I'll get to Heaven
and live with my Lord Jesus,
for all Eternity.

Eternal Home

Lord Jesus help me if You can,
help me be a better man,
change my life so I can be
a better follower of thee.
Each day I walk my life on earth
give me meaning, give me worth,
let me give a helping hand
until I reach the promised land,
then when I stand before the throne
I'll praise you for my Eternal home.

Chapter 5

THE FINAL CHAPTER

This final chapter of poems, once again shows us the importance of following and trusting Jesus. There Is No Price To pay for salvation and We Have Hope in the name of Jesus. We need not be afraid to stand alone for what we believe in. God's presence is always with us, guiding us thro Life's Storms until we reach our Heavenly home where we will spend Eternity with our wonderful friend and Saviour in the New Jerusalem. I trust and pray you have been blest as you read these poems and have come to a better understanding of our Lord Jesus and the plans He has for our lives here on earth and for Eternity in Heaven with Him.

No Price To Pay

With no eyes upon our precious Lord
no thoughts towards His precious word,
they start the day Him not in mind
stumbling forward as tho they're blind.
The arrows fly on each move they make
following the path in satan's wake,
hard the trial, temptations will,
struggling and striving up life's steep hill.
They carry the loads of worldly cares
the yoke is hard as they climb the stairs,
to reach a goal, they know not where
some may reach yet will not share.
The greed grows daily as riches mount
the stores are full yet there's no relent,
for most they struggle towards the day
when tired and weary they have to say.
I'm sick of all this toil and pain
I wish I had my life again.
There is an answer to all this woe,
let Jesus show you the way to go.
He'll take your load, the yoke He'll share,
He'll show you what it means to care
He'll give you all that you can bear,
a life in Him that you can trust
leading you towards that goal,
restoring mind, restoring soul.
Reach out your hand and have no fear,
let Jesus guide you on your way,
and once accepted in your heart,
you'll know there is no price to pay.

For All Battles Won

When we confess our Lord as Saviour
and to our lives He enters in,
then satan's fury comes against us
persuading us to stay in sin.
But we all know we have protection
in the name of Jesus Christ,
He died to save us all for Heaven
He rose to give us all new life.
Our bodies now a temple
sanctified by God's pure grace,
and we must keep this temple holy
until we meet Him face to face.

Because of this He gave us armour
for our protection from the world,
the shield of faith to stop the arrows
a helmet to protect His word.
A belt of truth our loins are girded,
sandals of peace our feet are shod,
a breastplate of righteousness firmly grounded
and the sword of the Spirit,
the Word of God.
So we must pray without ceasing
making known all our requests,
and praying for each other
the Saints and all the rest.
Then, as we are promised
His Word to fulfil,
He'll keep us all to Glory
to live out His will.

I do thank you my Father
and Jesus Christ your Son,
for the gift of your armour
and for all battles won.

We Have Hope

We have hope in the name of Jesus
when forsaken, when no-one else cares,
then it's time to surrender and call on His name
and He will answer and our troubles He'll share.
When people judge us, when friends scoff and scorn,
forgiveness comes through the shed blood of Jesus,
pierced by a cruel crown of thorns.
Turn now from the path that you walk on
turn now from the ways of the world,
cry out in the name of Jesus,
and believe in His wonderful word.
We have hope in the name of Jesus.

Or So It Seems

An hour, a day, a week, a year,
it matters not when Father makes it clear,
that every second day or night
He knows them all and keeps you in His sight.
But beware unless you fall or stray from narrow road,
stumble into darkness bearing heavy load.
Beware lest satan in his crafty guise,
entices you to follow and then to your surprise,
you are all alone, or so it seems, struggling, fighting,
helpless, carried by the torrent of life's raging streams,
washed away, nowhere to go, all is lost is this a dream.
Realities of life are sometimes hard to bear,
we stubbornly refuse Gods help, we stubbornly refuse
to share, until our hopes and dreams are gone
and we have no wish to carry on,
or so it seems.
But there within that darkest hour,
the graciousness of God His mercy shows,
and once again He guides us to His path
we stand amazed the love for us He proves.
From darkness into light He brings His guiding hand,
forgiveness He has shown,
forward onward, valiantly we go,
encouraged by God's Spirit, encouraged by our dreams.
New hope, new life, new goals,
we put our trust in God,
no more to say, or so it seems.

Don't Be Afraid

Don't be afraid to stand alone
believing that God created all we see.
Don't let man stand in your way
if you've got anything to say,
if Christ is real within your heart
then to the world His words impart.
Stand proud and tall, confess Him Lord,
profess you stand upon His word,
then when you meet Him face to face
He'll surely say you've earned a place
to spend with Me, as Gods intended all to be.

God's Presence

Where is God, He's here, He's there
His presence is all enveloping, He's everywhere.
No one more special, deserving of a favour
for each one known to God by name,
no rank, no position of high authority,
no one deserving fame.
For first the one who last shall be
and last the first in every case,
for God's love is plain to see
and He will see you face to face,
His love for all humanity.
In body soul and spirit find
our God, creator of you all,
the deaf, the dumb, the lame the blind
no one too big no one too small.
For omnipresent in the world
to all mankind He showed His love,
and sent His Son to prove His word
Isaiah spoke, foretold the truth.
So God is here in Spirit shown
and moves in ever present power,
and soon His Son will take you home
and on that day and in that hour,
the world will see the truth revealed
and Jesus by His presence shown,
will come to claim His very own.

Life's Storm

I sat and mused upon the day,
the wind blew hard and waves did rage
and rain lashed hard upon the window pane.
Yet still the peace within my heart
reminding me of God's pure grace,
the hand of certainty upon this place
and there I know with His command,
the raging of the storm will pass
and calm will once again return and we will rest.
Lord Jesus as we put our trust in You,
love us, bless us,
guard and protect us,
as You always do.
Amen.

Who Is God

Who is God? who is He?
God is all that we can see.
God is wind and rain and sun
He's been here since life began.
God is morning noon and night
He's the breath that gave us life,
God is comfort when in strife.
God is all that we can share
He's our strength so we can bear,
the times when trouble comes a calling
He's there to catch us when we're falling.
God is there when all seems lost
and he will never count the cost.
He will help and guide us thro each day
He's there to listen as we pray.
God will give us rest each night
He will help us make things right.
So God is special can't you see
He's always there for you and me.
God is perfect love and peace
and when one day when life will cease,
God will take us to His side
claiming all to be His bride.
Who is God? Who is He?
It's on that day that we will see.

Striving Onward

Do we know God's plan for us?
Is the future plain to see?
Are we called to move on forward?
Is this road for you and me?
Striving onward day by day,
trusting God will show the way,
knowing He will guide us on
to the goal He's set before us,
leading to our Eternal home

A Vision Of Heaven

In Heaven we're with the angels and those that's gone before
singing praises to our God and King, the one that we adore.
The light of Heaven is all around, bright shining as the stars,
the Sun the Moon and Jupiter and Capricorn and Mars.
Yet here the light shines from our Lord to brighten all our days
and for Eternity will shine as we worship Him and praise.
No more in sadness, toil, or pain, no sickness or disease,
no worries over anything just everything to please,
as we focus with the Heavenly host on God the Father and His Son,
praising the name of Jesus Christ who for us a victory won.
So if you think you're life, on earth, is all that you'll receive,
you only have to say these words, in God I do believe,
I open up my heart to You and ask You to come in,
I know that Jesus died for me, to take away my sin,
so when my life on earth is done please welcome me to Heaven,
to live and reign and sing your praises, with all of you forever.
Amen

Our Wonderful Friend

God gave us all things of great beauty,
the trees and the birds and the bees,
all wildlife is there for our pleasure
and all landscapes are what we perceive.
Lord God is our perfect Creator,
He made everything that we all see
and when birds sing melodious dawn chorus,
it fills all our lives with such glee.
Our Father, in Heaven, is our provider,
He'll clothe us and feed us good food,
He'll provide us with warmth and safe shelter
like a chicken with a newly hatched brood.
So trust Him, believe Him, revere Him
and when your life on this earth's at an end,
we'll claim our salvation with Jesus,
our Saviour and wonderful friend.

The New City Of Jerusalem

The streets of the New Jerusalem are pure gold and as transparent as glass,
the light from the glory of God makes it shine and the Lamb is the lamp, more Divine.
From God's throne and the Lamb's flows the river of life, down the middle of Great street, crystal clear, and the tree of life, stands each side, bearing fruit each month of the year.
The leaves of the tree heal the Nations and the walls of the city,
decorated with all precious stones, right down to the very foundations.
There is Jasper and Sapphire, Chalcedony and Emerald bright,
and Beryl and Topaz to name but a few, providing a wonderful sight.
The twelve gates round the walls, each one is a pearl, are placed in the stones round the city,
only those whose name's in the Lamb's book of life will go thro to live for Eternity.
So be ready, my friends, to enter that day, don't be left with the rabble outside,
having given your life to Jesus our Lord, for Eternity live by His side.

The Final Poem

This final poem I've written Lord
to give you thanks for the help you've given,
whilst meditating on Your written word
writing of an Eternal Heaven.
I've tried to show your Peace and Joy
but most of all your endless love,
which never fails, to all, you bring
because you are our Gracious Lord
with Perfect Understanding.

Read John 3 vs 16   and may God richly bless you.